THE COCKNEY POET

A First Selection of Poems by

CHARLES R. CLIFFORD

Published by Charles R. Clifford and Israel Renson
338 Victoria Park Road, E9.

ISBN 0 9508768 0 1
Printed by Lastcroft Ltd.,
5 Kingsbury Road, London N1 4AZ.

TO
ROSE

Foreword

Born in 1907, into a poor family, at Mile End in the East End of London, the author, Charles Clifford, experienced during childhood the extreme poverty conditions then prevailing in that area.

Despite domestic hardships, common to thousands of others, he regularly attended Ben Johnson Road School, Mile End, where he received his elementary education. However, he was not regarded as a good scholar.

He left school at fourteen to work as a "printer's devil", a very dirty job, which he soon exchanged for the hazardous occupation of selling newspapers on the streets.

In 1926 he joined the Army and was later sent to India. There he gained a First Class Certificate in Education, which was then unique for a farrier with the Royal Artillery. He also excelled at several sports including boxing, for which he won many trophies.

On leaving the Army he became a commissionaire and, in the spells between his duties, began to write poetry. When war broke out in 1939, as a reservist holding a First Class Education Certificate, he was offered a commission.

Having recently married and hence not relishing being posted to the Isle of St. Helena, he refused the offer. Instead he opted to become a Test Gunner at Woolwich Arsenal.

Returning after the war, with the rank of sergeant, to his former occupation as a commissionaire, the author later became first a grocer in Hackney, where he has lived for many years, and then a taxidriver.

His many hobbies, amongst them oil-painting, gardening and writing, give him much pleasure now that he is in his mid-seventies. Recently, he has temporarily set aside his art activities in order to concentrate on poetry. The fifty poems contained in this slim volume, which he hopes will appeal to many people, are but a small proportion of his total output. The author also hopes that readers will not hesitate to let him know their reactions to these "poems from the heart". He has many more awaiting publication which will depend upon the response to this first selection.

Although Charles Clifford describes himself as "The Cockney Poet" (and proud of it) his poems are not written in the cockney idiom. Rather, the term refers to his East End origin and upbringing.

Many of his poems reflect his love for his native city and for the motley medley of human characters that inhabit it. Others are inspired by his appreciation of Nature and the countryside. Some are concerned with love, with human fellowship, with contentment, harmony and the peace which is so elusive in this tumultuous world while a few are short verbal vignettes portraying personal memories of incidents from his past life.

Finally (and thankfully), his verses all possess a property which so often is lacking from much modern poetry. Happily they do rhyme.

Israel Renson. February 1983

Contents

What know they of London?

What know they of London Town
Who were never here to see?
What know they of London pride
Who were never born of thee?
What know they of Father Thames
Who ride not on his crest?
What know they of London men
Who have never faced the test?
Those little things that make our town
Endeared to young and old,
Like age-old Changing of the Guard
In scarlet and in gold,
The Whispering Gallery of St. Paul's
Its statues and the Dome,
The fountains in Trafalgar Square
Where pigeons make their home,
A hundred other things to see
In London Town to-day,
They draw the errant Cockney back,
When wandering on his way;
Some people laugh and some make fun
At London's passing shows,
But what know they of joy and tears
As only London knows?

The Spirit of Content

I wish I could an haven find,
    Where mankind dwells with peaceful mind,
Who cares not he for power nor pelf,
    Yet loves his neighbour as himself.

Then with my good ship Argosy,
    I'd sail my craft across the sea,
And for their spirit of content,
    I'd barter our world's betterment.

When

When you get to know the 'Knowledge' and know it like your hand,
    Then pass out in a taxi, from Lambeth to the Strand,
When you suffer many heartaches and your dreams of fortune fade
    And you learn by hard experience how money's truly made,
When you can ignore cabbies, that sit in "caffs" all day,
    Who go home in the evening with hardly any pay,
When you get to wasting diesel, from the Elephant to the Zoo,
    Have the luck of 'nine blind beggars' and get to Waterloo,
When up at 'Dilly Circus', with the traffic at its worst,
    You pick up from young Eros, with a taxi that's been cursed,
When cruising in the evening before the clock strikes ten,
    Trap one up to Euston, then get one back agen,
When you wait for several hours, on a rank that has no end,
    With thoughts of cab repayments and a 'dodgy' rear big end,
When you go home really happy, though your takings have been light,
    With the smell of stale cigar smoke, drifting through the night,
When you suffer these things gladly and take them on the run,
    You'll be as good a man as I am — you'll be a Taxidriver, son!

Early Dawn

Grey streaks across a tinted sky,
    Fresh to my face the breath of morn,
Then out of doors alone go I,
    To hear the sounds of early dawn.

I note the violets in the glade,
    With the scent of dew-soaked clay,
I see the fox slink to the shade,
    To seek his lair at start of day.

As softly on the leaves I tread,
    I hear a skylark sing,
Through some branches overhead,
    I spot his speckled wing.

With startled fright some creatures small,
    At my intrusion peep,
No need for fear, I love them all,
    So to the path I keep.

From a pinetree scented covert,
    I hear the cooing of the dove,
Across the vale o'er castle turret,
    Where the mist does rise above.

In the blushing of day's dawning,
    Creeps a badger stealthily,
But I find myself ayawning,
    So home to breakfast, toast and tea.

The Sky's the Limit

Here is a tale of a berserk age,
    With nuclear fission all the rage;
A statesman says, with tongue in cheek,
    That the size of *his* bomb has reached its peak,
No bigger ones will then be used,
    He hopes his faith is not abused;
But how will an enemy know the size,
    As destruction falls from out the skies?
Let's try a small one, some fool will say,
    On some future drastic day;
Who then will care how much it weighs
    When the thing's a nuclear haze?

Will the enemy weigh the ounce,
    When they start their bomb to bounce?
With hydrogen missile to blast the earth,
    To annihilate and scorch the turf,
Which may bring e'en a greater shock,
    Vaporising hills and granite rock,
In a flash that nuclear fission,
    Which started out with mild derision,
May blast this planet from the skies
    Into the Universe, atomised.

Early Morning in May

From my window, when I rise,
        I see a skylark in the skies,
Then I know the day is fine again;
        As a swallow from the eaves,
Darts amid the laurel leaves,
        Scattering dew like summer rain.

A blackbird from the hedgerow sings,
        Mellow notes and his echo rings,
When this day is newly born,
        Comes the furtive rabbit, on the lea,
Out from his burrow lazily,
        To trespass on my lawn.

The early roses kissed with dew,
        With their fragrance sweet and new,
In my garden greet the day,
        Enticing now the bumble bee,
That comes abuzzing busily,
        In this pleasant month of May.

Our Island Home

Where soars the warbling skylark high
        In a hazy summer's sky,
O'er ripening corn and meadows green,
        Shallow, murmuring, pleasant stream.

Where sunsets turn the dusk to fire,
        Tinting trees and castle spire,
As lowing cattle wend their way
        To the farm at the end of the day.

Where towering oak and stately pine
        Scent the air like fragrant wine,
With heather-covered rolling downs,
        Far from city or smoky towns.

Where chalky cliffs run to the beaches,
        A little church where parson preaches,
Our island home, where all are free,
        As near to heaven as one could be.

Missing You

I've missed you so these last few days,
    I've missed those eyes with sunshine rays,
I've missed your laugh with tinkling tones,
    You've left me, now I'm all alone.

To know you cared made me so proud,
    So now I dwell upon a cloud,
When coming back again to earth,
    I feel enslaved, a bonded serf.

Hearth and home have beckoning calls,
    The firelight flickers as daylight falls,
To dwell in dreams must be for me,
    A world wherein I find ecstasy.

Must I always live with dreams
    Where lovers woo by moonlit streams?
I'd like to think of cosy cots,
    A happy home and copper pots.

When you return to me again,
    I'll be relieved from grief and pain,
For I am happy when you are near me,
    You are the one that I love dearly.

The Chalet

In the chalet by the white cliff side
    Where lovers ofttimes go,
We heard the roar of the waves and tide,
    Which were raging far below.

There I sat with my Rosemarie,
    We saw the moon ride high,
Content was I and so was she,
    Then the time to leave was nigh.

Those bygone years when I was young,
    With Rosie by my side,
We pledged our love in that chalet high,
    O'er the roar of the raging tide.

Now my love has gone, in my muse I hear
    Cries of the gulls that soared
O'er the chalet we held so dear,
    With the darling I adored.

The Song of the Wheels

In the early hours of morning,
    Now my hours of duty o'er,
I'm heading for my homestead
    And travelling East once more.
'Clickity clackity, clickity clackity'
    The call of the road to the wheels,
'Clickity clackity, clickity clackity,'
    A man's as young as he feels.

As the miles go flying past,
    In these early hours of day,
In my mind a tune is cast,
    For the wheels, they seem to say;
    'Clickity clackity, clickity clackity'
    The call of the road to the wheels,
'Clickity clackity, clickity clackity'
    A man's not so young as he feels.

When you're young and you're foolish,
    You want to burn up the road,
When you're older and mulish,
    You tend to ease on your load.
'Clickity clackity, clickity clackity'
    The call of the road to the wheels,
'Clickity clackity, clickity clackity'
    A man's as old as he feels.

Wishful Thinking

Could I get back all my yesterdays
And change them for tomorrows,
Could I plan the future better
To leave behind the sorrows,
Then each brick that built my castles,
Would be quite firm and strong,
All my dreams of conquest
Could never then go wrong.

Now we know that mortar crumbles
And human flesh decays,
So what's the use of wishing
For bygone wasted days?
We've each at some time moulded,
As every minute passed,
Our futures and of others
For whom the die is cast.

We cannot erase memories
Nor hold the past to scorn,
For each event was destined
Since ere the world was born.
I'll not regret my yesterdays
Although that some were grey,
I'll face the future stronger
Knowing it's God's own way.

When I Retire

Maybe one day when I retire
And I can sit out on the lawn,
Perhaps I'll find my heart's desire,
The peace we seek from the day we're born.

If death should come when I'm alone,
Then none will hear my solemn prayer,
But if around are loved ones known.
So I'll say to kinsfolk there,

"God bless you all, and may He care,
For all on earth from high above,
Let all loved ones troubles share,
For family life is based on Love".

The Sweetest Rose

Of all the great ladies wherever they are,
I think that my Rose is the sweetest by far,
I call her my sweetheart and she knows in her heart
That nothing nor anyone could keep us apart;
Of wealth I've few pennies, few treasures I own,
Still my Rose is the equal to a queen on a throne,
Yet if I've but pennies, another asset I hold,
I have Rose's affection, it's worth more than red gold,
So with her charms so beguiling, a pleasure indeed,
I've the prettiest flower, all the treasure I need.

Dunkirk Beaches, 1940

That night as we lay
    on a bleak foreign strand
With scarcely a star keeping
    watch o'er the earth,
The drone of the planes
    from our dear native land
Turned our thoughts to old England
    the land of our birth.

How soon would I see
    the home dear to me,
With but a few miles
    to keep us apart,
In my mind's eye
    my wife I could see,
Calling and praying
    to keep a stout heart.
Weeks of hard fighting
    with backs to the wall,
The Germans broke through us
    to pillage and plunder,
But our Air Force and Navy
    now answered our call,
The noise of their gunfire
    sounded like thunder.

Now we were lying
    on Dunkirk's flat strand,
Awaiting the dawn
    and rescue by boats,
Looking and yearning
    for the sight of our land,
While cries from the wounded
    raised lumps in our throats.

That night seemed the longest
that ever I knew,
With death all around us
in low tones we spoke,
Then as the dawn lightened
our hopes grew and grew,
From the brave soldiers
resounding cheers broke.
With ships on the skyline
was a host of small fry,
Boats from the backstreams
from the lakes and the bays.
They had come to our succour,
no need to ask why,
We'll remember them always,
for the rest of our days.

They ferried us homewards from war, and the din,
From Dunkirk's flat beaches in dawn's early light,
We were defeated in battle but with stout hearts within
Knowing that someday we'd return to the fight.

Priceless Love

Priceless is my darling, loving me so,
Best of all treasures one could bestow,
She wears no fine jewels, but what do I care,
I'm happy, contented, yet no millionaire.

I cannot be poor when there's gold in her hair,
For there in her eyes are diamonds all rare,
And then when I hold her so close in my arms,
I'm really quite rich with the wealth of her charms.

Stephen and I

When schooldays were over and holidays nigh,
    Off on a picnic went Stephen and I,
In our pockets were sandwiches, some apples too,
    That Mother had packed, with toffees to chew;
As we ran down the lane that led to the moor,
    We noticed the haycart by farmer Jones' door,
So we clambered aboard the single horse dray,
    To snuggle down quietly 'neath the fresh hay;
With a flick of his whip when farmer Jones saw,
    He woke us both up by the village pub door,
Then down by the river on our backs we did lie,
    Fishing and eating, just Stephen and I.

When our idling was finished, sun high in the sky,
    Off to the forest went Stephen and I,
Climbing great oak trees, beeches as well,
    We'd startle the squirrels by giving a yell,
Acting like Indians, to a glade we would creep,
    Hoping to catch a young rabbit to keep,
Then spying a tramp, from the forest we'd run,
    To hold our sides laughing because it was fun,
Now down by the pond near the village we spied
    The clump of bullrushes where moorhens did hide,
So home past the farmyard with pigs in their sty,
    Holding our noses came Stephen and I.

When sunset's red streakers came tinting the sky,
    We'd sort all our conkers, Stephen and I,
Then wander home slowly, the sun in the west,
    And slash at the thistles, as high as our chest,
We'd mock at the night owl, its call loud and clear,
    Then duck down our heads when a bat came quite near,
We'd talk in a whisper of fairies and ghosts,
    And pretend to be frightened at the sight of a post,
With our house now in view, Mother there too,
    Waiting to scold us as all mothers do,
We got to our gate with a laugh and a sigh,
    Then to bed, tired and happy, went Stephen and I.

Boyish Dreams

Beneath a shady maple tree, with quietly grazing sheep,
The shepherd boy has dropped his book, lies gently, fast asleep.
The fairy tale of long ago, with dragon's eyes agleam,
Forgotten, lies upon the grass, as he begins to dream;
He dreams of towns and city streets, lighted shops and stores,
While all around him, in his dream, the noisy traffic roars.

Beneath a laden coster barrow, in a London market street,
Lies a ragged Cockney urchin, a mongrel at his feet,
He dreams of lush and grassy meadows, with grazing sheep o'er dales,
In mind's eye the skylark flies, to soar o'er hills and vales,
Then, like the shepherd boy, he wakes to do a task they know,
Both dreaming forth to another world, as on through life they go.

New Year's Eve

On New Year's Eve, when the day departs
And the old year fades into the aged past,
We welcome the new with eager hearts,
Hoping it provides us with peace to last.

A peace that to our babes may bring
A fellowship o'er the world to span,
No thoughts of avarice nor enmity cling,
No time for self but for everyman.

Coronation Day, 1953

There's a murmur from the teeming crowd,
    The Palace gates are opened wide,
Emerging forth the Horse Guards proud,
    There's the carriage with the Queen inside.

Along the Mall the people wait
    To see their Queen in regal gown,
At the Abbey heads of state
    Are waiting now to set the Crown.

Oath and prayer now are ended,
    Subjects at their monarch stare
Now the regal knee is bended,
    See the circlet in her hair.

Elizabeth the Second now is crowned,
    Her banner full unfurled,
The news is soon passed all around
    To the peoples of the world.

The welkin rings "God bless the Queen"
    Loud peal bells far and wide,
Long may she reign and live supreme,
    The symbol of old England's pride.

Slowly forth with stately mien,
    The Queen now to her carriage goes,
Full robed Her Majesty then is seen,
    Guards and escorts on their toes.

'Midst the pomp and grand array
    The Queen drives through her London Town,
Bedecked with flags and bunting gay,
    Lampposts adorned with gilded crown.

With martial air and stirring march,
    The cavalcade nears St. James,
Turreted walls with gothic arch,
    Where dwelt the Royals with famous names.

Now at last the Queen arrives
    At Buckingham's home of majesty,
With her escort also drives
    The Consort with their family.

Around the gates crowds are surging,
    Waiting for their Queen to see,
Soon with Consort seen emerging
    Step they to the balcony.

Long and loud the people call,
    For the Royal-Apparent Heir,
Then the multitude in the Mall,
    See the Prince with parents there.

Then at last with duty done,
    The Queen to stateroom makes her way,
Leaving her subjects to their fun,
    On England's own Coronation Day.

The Strange Beggar

I awoke one morn when the day was new,
I'd had a dream that was with me still,
I dreamed that I was of the chosen few,
Who had tended Jesus on a distant hill.

The Lord had told me in my dream,
That he'd visit me that very day;
I at once began to dust and clean
The rooms in which the Lord would stay.

I swept and polished all day and sang
Because my heart was light and gay,
I went to the door when the bell had rang,
But it was only a beggar in poor array.

I chased him away from my step so clean,
He smiled at me as he left the door,
Then I saw the mark where his feet had been,
And hurried to clean the step once more.

I washed and scrubbed with might and main,
Yet I could not shift that stranger's mark,
It seemed this was a magic stain,
I gave up when the skies grew dark.

All night my eyes were full of tears,
No word from the Lord now day was done,
What had gone wrong? I was full of fears,
Why had he failed me, the Holy One?

That night the Lord appeared again,
He gave a smile but, alas, was sad,
I asked him why he never came,
He answered that he really had.

"That beggar man" replied the Lord,
"You turned away, so poor was he
Inasmuch as you refused him board
You also did it unto me".

Delights of London

To feed the birds in Trafalgar Square,
    To feel the spray of the fountains there,
To sit by the lake in Regent's Park,
    To watch the kids by the Serpentine,
These are some delights of mine,
    In London before it's dark.

After dark, it's my delight
    To stand near Eros where all is bright,
Watching folk all smart and gay,
    They dine in Soho or Mayfair grand
Or in the bistros off the Strand,
    Then to theatres at end of day.

On Sundays fine I go to the Zoo,
    As many other people do,
To watch the ape and chimpanzee,
    They leap and jump into the air
Then at us folk they sit and stare
    Whilst sipping cups of tea.

Other delights are there for all,
    Museums and the music hall,
Yet my delight on a rainy day
    When all around is dismal wet
    With seats at cinema hard to get,
Is to go where the big stores lay.

Thoughts of Home

So oft I stray in fancy's muse
    Across a pleasant lea,
To seek the wild plants' varied hues
    Where sucks the bumble bee.

There I see in my dreaming mind,
    Like a mirage o'er the sand,
Sun-flecked clouds, a golden hind,
    And heather-covered land.

At other times my mind portrays
    A scene where fountains spring,
With gardens in a summer's haze,
    A house where roses cling.

In my muse I seem to see
    My loved ones all around,
With Stephen dangling on my knee
    And Andrew on the ground.

My dear wife to caress me kneels
    To chase my cares this day,
Thoughts of home come flooding still,
    Although I'm far away.

When Winter Comes

When winter o'er the meadow creeps,
Her mantle there to spread,
I pray the shepherd safely keeps
The cattle to their shed.

With snowdrifts thick upon the hill,
There's a lamb that's wandered o'er,
I pray the shepherd has the skill
To find the stray once more.

When winter feels the breath of spring,
With warm sun breaking through,
The shepherd now is seen to bring
His flock of lambs quite new.

Father, Mother and I

Oh, happy the days when we played on the sands,
Many the castles we made with our hands,
Shrimping and paddling with donkey rides too,
Still laughing at Punch as if it were new;
A penny to look at the ships passing by,
Never happier were Father, Mother and I.

White were our faces as the sailing boat heeled,
We laughed at the pigs in their sty as they milled,
Now that our snapshots memories retain,
We still hear the seagulls and waves roar again,
To think of those good days we each give a sigh,
Each to our thoughts, Father, Mother and I.

The Poppy

Poppies in the cornfield born,
    Their splash of colour seen
Against the golden ears of corn,
    Amid the fields so green.

The cycle of events does show,
    As ears of corn are sown,
Their tiny shoots begin to grow,
    When to the earth they're thrown.

Now 'twixt those shoots are tiny weeds
    Which to their end must grow,
Then in fulfilment of their needs,
    Into the wind they go.

Now the gentle earth does yield again,
    The poppies are but weeds,
They harvest then the golden grain,
    To grind the wheaten seeds,

The Poppy in the field of corn,
    The pleasant gold to violate,
Will every year again be born,
    With fragile robe incarnate.

Don't sit back

When you're close to five and sixty
    With your life of toil near done,
Don't just sit in quiet retirement
    But take your share of fun;
You don't have to watch the kiddies
    Once they're off your hands;
Go away for long excursions
    To the country or the sands;
You can't hope to climb a mountain
    Or captain a football match,
But you can keep the brainbox working
    Though it's under old grey thatch,
Then when you're well nigh eighty,
    With yet another span in view,
You'll have lived your life more ably,
    With the doctor's visits few.

The Glade

Where the glade is quiet and cool,
    Where the brook runs to the pool,
Where the trees in all their glory,
    Remind me of love, that old, old story.
The love that came to us in May,
    When into the glade we chanced to stray.

We vowed each then to the other's heart,
    That from that hour we ne'er would part;
We carved our names on a tree that grew
    In the glade when our love was new,
The love that came to us in May,
    When into the glade we chanced to stray.

Now autumn leaves have turned to gold,
    Our plighted troth has failed to hold,
We're parted now, but down memory lane,
    My thoughts of love will long remain,
Of the love that came to us in May,
    When into the glade we chanced to stray.

Fatal Time

If I could carve a huge, hard rock
To last until some future stage,
I'd carve an image like a clock
That scourged us in this age.

We foolish folk, the Human Race
All try to beat the sun,
Quicker, faster goes the pace
Until a thing is done.

My message carved, long time to last,
Would be like a picture bold,
Future age could know the past
So read the symbols told.

I'd tell the future earthly race,
If they could understand,
How man was sent to outer space,
To settle time's demand.

We humans in our race with time,
Now all the world is spanned,
Like birds with wings we soar and climb
To seek in space for other land.

Gone is the peace and quiet of life,
For time was made by knaves,
To find a world that's free from strife,
Is to find it in our graves.

London Cemeteries

What are you now, you heap of stones,
    Wherein your ancients lie?
What use are you whose dust is sown
    Upon the passer-by?

You clutter up the narrow road
    With the smell of damp decay,
Your space could ease the worker's load
    When his tasks are done each day.

What use are names like Brown or Jones
    Or Smith or Peter, too?
For all that's left is dust and bones
    Of those remembered few.

Your job is done, you've served us well,
    Make way for youth and love,
We need your space wherein to dwell
    With the symbol of the dove.

A Run in the Park

At the side of the lake
    With the mist rising high,
The hour before breakfast
    Went Scampy and I.
The sound of his barking
    As he chased the wild hen
Would echo the woodlands,
    Then down to the glen,
With my dog out of sight
    I would whistle his call.
From the mist would bounce Scampy
    Like a big, fluffy ball,
Then homewards we'd wander
    To Mum, home and hearth,
Crossing the meadow
    By a well-trodden path,
The smell of fresh coffee
    With bacon and eggs,
Would give a fresh spirit
    And a spring to my legs,
With a laugh and a bark
    We would run to the door,
Then Scampy would know that
    His outing was o'er.

A Wintry Dawn

The settled white of a snowy street
As dawn breaks through the sky,
Then the prints of a motley thousand feet,
When the crowds go hurrying by.
The huddled form in a doorway curled,
With a mongrel by her side,
Driftwood from a madcap world,
A vagrant without pride;
As the sun comes up on that wintry scene
The snowflakes cease to fall,
With muffled tread and casual mien
A policeman moves her shawl;
The mongrel growls at the policeman's touch
But the huddled form is still,
On haggard face that suffered much
Cruel death had paid the bill;
As they tried to take the dog away
The cur it fought and snarled,
Then licked the face so worn like clay,
With hands so thin and gnarled;
In a pauper's grave unmarked and bare
In a corner scarcely known,
They laid the beggar woman where
The weeds had thickly grown;
They took the dog to a stray dogs' home,
Like its mistress then found rest
No longer would they have to roam
In the streets that they loved best;
Now in the slush of a London street
As dawn breaks in the sky,
Other tramps are on the beat
Of a policeman passing by.

Perhaps

I ofttimes wish that I had made
My life as a sailor on the sea,
To sail the world and seek the trade
For coffee, timber, spice or tea.

Then again sometimes I think I might
Have made a dashing soldier too,
Seeking glory in the fight,
Wearing clothes of red and blue.

Yet then again perhaps I may
Have dug for treasure or hidden gold,
Dug up objects in the clay
Or fathomed secrets ages old.

Still, now the spark of youth is ended
I have not now the urge to roam,
With mellow age and wisdom blended
My place is now with hearth and home.

True Love

If one could have riches with diamonds galore,
You could still be unhappy without love at your door,
Money can't buy it nor monarchs bestow,
Love's sent from heaven to mortals below.

Like the love of a mother when her baby is born,
Or the love of a maiden when youth is forlorn,
Like the love of a dear one who cannot be near,
Or love for your country, the one that's so dear.

An Only Son

Why can't the Lord a brother send
So I can have some fun?
My little dog is just a friend,
For I'm an only son.

When I go out with Mum and Dad,
I know they're very kind,
But my little dog is very glad
When he has pals to find.

I love my folks quite lots and lots,
They love me too, I know,
But what they need is many cots
With nappies in a row.

My little pal lies near my bed,
I stroke him when I wake,
He licks my hand, I pat his head,
When our breakfast we partake.

I give my pal small tasty tips
When Mother is not near,
He wags his tail, licks his lips,
His actions I love dear.

When I grow up I hope to see,
My own boys having fun,
Thanks to God and thanks to me,
There'll be no only son.

The Daisy Chain

If all the wealth of London Town
Were thrown down at my feet,
It could not match that regal crown
You made of daisies sweet.

When hand in hand we made our way
Across the pleasant lea,
I remember well that lovely day
With the view of the distant sea.

We sat awhile without a care,
Some daisy chains we made,
You placed the flowers in my hair,
That day our love was made.

You never knew that daisy ring
I keep with my treasures now,
And from my album often cling
Those flowers to my brow.

Although the years have passed me by,
My love will still remain
And be the same until I die,
With my faded daisy chain.

When the Circus came

When I was but a little boy
I thought the circus grand,
One thing I know I did enjoy,
The sound of the big brass band.

Laughing at a clown's droll play,
Would cause my sides to ache,
I held my breath as he failed to stay
On the tightrope all ashake.

The lions and tigers with the bears
Caused my heart to give a leap
When the tamer set them on some chairs,
And then snarling to their sleep.

Later when the show was o'er,
With the stars set in the sky,
Happy and tired it was home once more
Where I heaved a great big sigh.

Sometimes I gave a helping hand,
To make the tentropes tight,
My favourite job was to sprinkle sand
For the ring on opening night.

Then loading the wagons, on the move once more,
I'd follow them down the lane,
Just to hear the animals roar,
When the tractors took the strain.

Now every year, when the time comes round,
I still run to our garden gate,
As I hear from afar the welcome sound
Of my good old circus mate.

Our Annual Holiday

Off in the car when August came
Playing with dad the 'I spy' game,
Through the town and busy streets,
Lots of snacks with cake and sweets,
As the miles go flying by,
We see a rainbow in the sky,
On our annual holiday.

Then days of leisure, azure seas,
Fields and meadows, shady trees,
Far from all the city madness,
Away from all the gloom and sadness,
Happy hours of peace and pleasure,
Times for all to ever treasure.
On our annual holiday.

The Truant

Bending reeds in rushing stream,
A wellthrown line from a bank,
Time to laze and time to dream,
Until the hook with fish had sank.

The country life was the one for me,
For such I knew as a boy,
Now years go by and I seem to see
My schooldays full of joy.

As the schoolbell rang from old belltower
With sun bright in the sky,
I'd linger and idle away the hour,
With my school pals hurrying by.

So late I'd find the schooldoor closed,
To the river I found my way,
There I sat with rod and dozed
Until the ending of the day.

My father coming home to tea
Would lots of questions ask,
I hung my head, prepared to be
A truant taken to task.

With extra work that came to me
For being such a fool,
I learned the lesson not to be
A truant away from school.

The Story Teller

I recall the tales my father told
    Of the good old days of yore,
With pirates bold and hidden gold
    Of cannon, blood and gore;
He made believe and used to rove,
    Like Long John Silver did,
To find the cove with treasure trove
    Of bad old Captain Kidd.
With Morgan and his cutthroat crew,
    He sailed for the Spanish Main,
There were fights and captures by our lads in blue,
    Then we moved on once again.

My father told of bold Robin Hood
    Who had men in green array,
He did much good in old Sherwood,
    Wherein their story lay;
Many were the tales that father knew
    Of giants and castles tall,
Some were false but some were true,
    Still, I really loved them all.
Now if I can tell my children things
    That father once told me,
Then I may match his angel wings,
    To live for eternity.

Epping Forest

Epping Forest, old London's pride,
Where cockney children love to hide
Among the trees in sport and play,
Shouts of laughter the livelong day.

Freckled boy with face repining,
Clutching jar with newts reclining,
White-aproned girl with daisies crowned,
Enthroned on wishing-clover ground.

Tall beeches sway in woodland shade,
Leafy bowers and pleasant glade,
Haunts of squirrel, red and grey,
Kestrel, starling, owl and jay.

Near pond, in thicket hiding,
Fearing man on footpath riding,
Fallow deer with offspring panting,
Making scene fore'er enchanting.

Of all the places one could see
To dwell in peace and harmony,
If I could hope to live forever
I'd choose that realm of fern and heather.

Youth Recalled

Oft as I sit engrossed in thought,
I bring to mind the life I wrought,
The days of joys and sorrows too,
As I from boy to manhood grew,

From lowly hearth at mother's knee,
I ran the streets at the age of three,
Then later came the school and play,
No cares had I the livelong day.

The thud of boot, a lifting ball,
A rush to climb o'er the garden wall,
Those boyhood hours are with me still.
They bind me fast-they always will.

Then, in mind's eye, I see a pool,
Where we would swim soon after school,
A rod and line with shady tree,
No homework then for lazy me.

We envied not the well-dressed boys,
Those who played with expensive toys,
Our games were all of boyish fun,
To swim and skip, to leap and run.

Where now are those dear friends I knew?
The poor, ragged kids with whom I grew?
Some may be dead but still they'll be
In my memories for eternity.

Old Chinatown

When you're at the Pump by Aldgate East,
Then travel down to Charlie Brown's,
There you'll see the dregs, to say the least,
Migrants from the worldwide towns.

They settled here from East and West,
From old Shanghai and Tokio,
Like ants emerging from seething nest,
So did this Chinatown grow.

Now old Chang Wong lived in Chinatown,
The toughest spot they say,
And with him lived, in flowered gown,
His daughter, young Kim May.

This Chinese girl was near seventeen,
Always filling the air with song,
Pressing and ironing in the laundry clean,
Of her father, the old Chang Wong.

Then one dark night by Wapping Wall,
When the fog was thick around,
They heard a scream, a stifled call,
From a figure on the ground.

A girl they found, raped and dead,
When the sun came through next day,
Far and wide, the news was spread,
Of the death of young Kim May.

They never caught that wretched beast
Who did that ghastly deed,
So old Chang Wong went back home East,
To live with his Chinese breed.

They often speak to this very day,
Of the girl in the flowered gown,
The laundry girl called young Kim May,
The pride of old Chinatown.

A New Champion

When the poisoned barbs of critics sting
With much censure as the idol falls,
Where once the arena with acclaim did ring,
Now echo acrimonious, jeering calls.

I once sipped the nectar of glorious days.
When, crowned as victor, I conquered all,
To collect the garlands from the dais,
With many trophies to adorn my wall.

No more to battle and share the sport
Which youth with all its vigour gains,
No more to flirt with fate so short,
For a new and younger champion reigns.

The Oldest Inhabitant

I may be ninety years or more
    But still I get about,
I hobble from my cottage door
    To get my pint of stout;
And as I sit upon the bench
    Outside the village inn,
I see the sportive lad and wench
    Drinking at the bar within.

Few now the faces that once I knew
    Before the reaper made his call,
For many are here with faces new
    Within our village small;
I remember Tom, the farmer's hand,
    How he could quaff his ale!
He knew the way to plough the land
    O'er the upland or the dale;

Bertie Clark lies in the shade
    Beneath the graveyard here,
Few flowers on his mound were laid,
    For no one shed a tear;
Last Sunday when the parson prayed,
    In church across the way,
I helped the organist who played
    The harvest hymns that day;
Then as I pumped that organ weak,
    By squire's respected bust,
I peeped around the side to seek
    A nip to lay the dust;

I often chuckle o'er my beer
To see the madcap pace,
The speed of cars that pass through here,
Those follies of the human race;
Now I'm contented with my lot,
With a grandchild at my knee,
For what's in store I know not what,
But what's good for Him suits me.

Destiny

My wife was sighing as women can,
"It's alright for you. You're a man"
So I replied, "It's God's own plan,
And so it's been since the world began".

"For if I were you and you were me,
I wonder where we now would be.
Hitched to a star too far to see,
Or lost in a sea of calamity?"

"I think my dear, we must agree
That what does happen is meant to be;
Throughout our lives we cannot see
To our ultimate end-our destiny".

The Test of a Man

What's the good of a man when in battle
If he's scared and weak at the knees?
And then in a crisis his nerves rattle
With panic in his efforts to please.

What's the use of a man who keeps wailing
And can't face the music when whipped?
Then makes all excuses for failing
As right on the target gets pipped.

What's the good of a man when he's chosen
For honours but fails at the test,
When the game for the game's sake has proven
That a loser is often the best?

There's much pleasure in winning but think on,
The prize does not seem quite the same,
If the one who had won made a bargain
With the loser the garland to claim.

What's the use of a man who's not trying?
Devoid of ambition and hope
When all those around him are dying
And he feels at the end of his rope.

A man's not a man when he's cringing
Or thinking of self all the while,
For the test of a man is the bringing
Of succour to others, without guile.

So what's the use of those weak men at all
If they can't stand up to a fight,
Making a stand with backs to the wall,
Or a problem in life that is tight?

The Water-Cart

I remember well the water-cart,
When it came round on a summer's day;
We were young, happy and gay at heart
As we skipped midst the gentle spray;

The carter's whip we'd dodge with ease
For we had no shoes to wear,
With shouts of glee, the man to tease,
We asked just the spray to share;

Then when he stopped to fill his cart
And watch us angrily,
We'd wait again for him to start,
Then chase him warily.

The day of the water-cart's long gone past,
And the time of the horses o'er,
But now in memories, long to last,
I see those carts, once more.

Tower of London Gardens

Here once the feet of traitors paced,
But now there's peace and rest,
I sat and watched while children raced,
Till the sun set in the west.

I watched the kiddies with grownups on
The cannons of the Tower,
And soldiers changing guard upon
The gates at every hour.

Then Tower Bridge went up to let
Big steamers from the sea,
Some small tugs, with their hawsers set,
Pulled barges full of tea.

I saw a naughty urchin swim,
All naked from the beach,
The river police then spotted him,
But he was quickly out of reach.

I sat and fed the birds with bread,
Starlings and sparrows small,
And the gulls, flying overhead,
Gave such a screeching call.

From a very hard seat I see the pier,
With the pigeons soaring over,
The paddle steamers go from here,
To Windsor and to Dover.

When at last the day does fade
The garden bell is tolled,
I wander homewards up the grade,
Where traitors' heads once rolled.

The Sea Shell

Close your eyes, my daughter dear,
Hold this shell close to your ear.
Can you hear the sound of waves?
The roaring sea o'er sailors' graves?
Now shut your eyes and pretend to be
A shipwrecked mariner on the sea
His raft has grated on the sand
Of some uncharted foreign land.

Keep your eyelids fastened yet,
Now the sailor, gaunt and wet,
Staggers forth upon the strand,
Surrounded by a heathen band.
Still for a short while close your eyes,
Then in your mind just visualise
Those painted warriors now giving aid,
With all their help and rescue made.
Open your eyes now, you must break the spell,
It's my turn now for the pretty sea shell.

On London Bridge

See the motley, jostling crowd,
    Like ants from nest emerging,
Note the anxious and the proud,
    Now on the streets all surging.

Daily to their tasks they go,
    Each to a joy pretending,
Tycoon, typist, high and low,
    Each on their skill depending.

As I mingle with the throng,
    That comes from the station early,
I often hear a barrow-boy's song,
    Amidst the hurly-burly.

If one could make each face portray,
    What would we find revealing?
That youngster with a tie so gay,
    Was overnight sad, grieving.

The dandy with the hurried pace,
    His domestic strife surmounting,
Will ere the darkness find disgrace,
    With former friends so doubting.

Some idlers watching o'er the Pool
    Ships now fast unloading,
There seated on his office stool
    Is a clerk at work, decoding.

All very well for lazy louts
    Who over the bridge keep peeping,
But I can't linger hereabouts,
    As my time for work is creeping.